to make

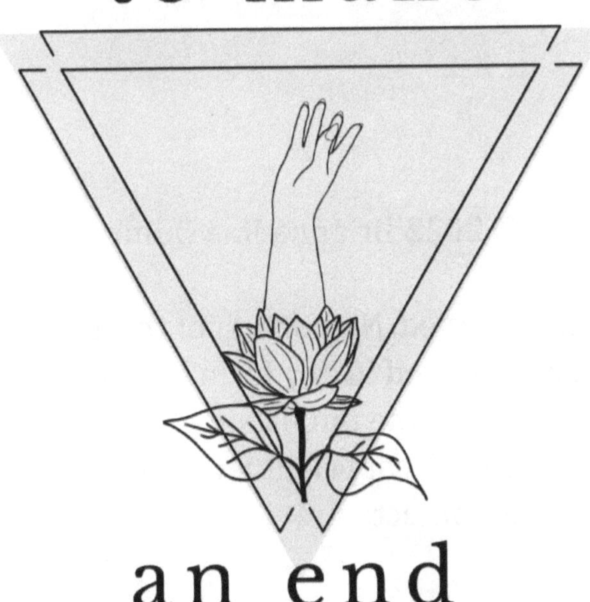

an end

This book is dedicated Chrissy, who always waters my roots.

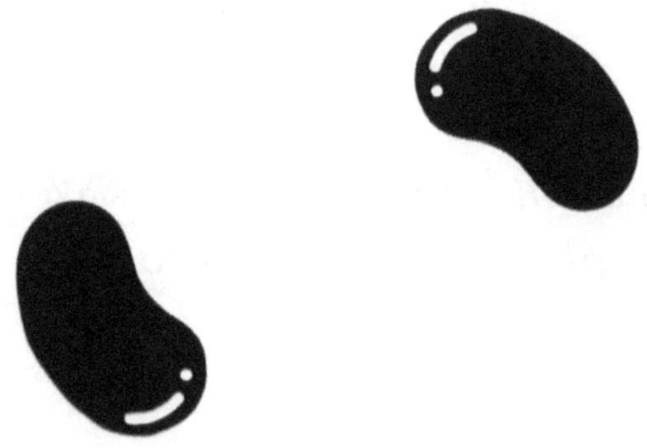

"For last year's words belong to last year's language, and next year's words await another voice, and to make an end is to make a beginning."

— *T.S. Eliot*

Table of Contents

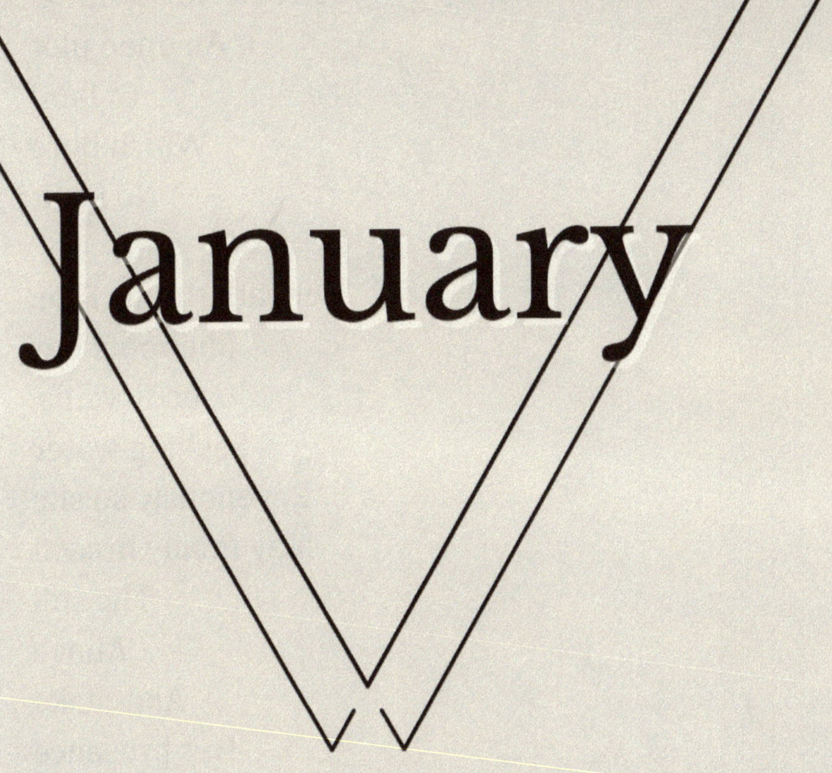
Beginnings
January
Duality

beginnings

Seedling
From the surface,
She shows nothing;
An open plot
Of land
Which bore
No fruit.

Beneath the surface,
She roots her
Greedy veins,
Seeking water
Ravenously so she
May finally breach
The soil
Above
And make
Her presence
Known.

Drowning
I've never grasped at nothing
So desperately.
I had taken the air for granted.
She had given me so much
Wonder in life.
Kicking wildly to ascend from
A watery plane,
To inhale the sweet
Flavor of pure wind,
I know
She cannot save me from
Sinking;
Intangible, like faith.

But each wave that crashes
Overhead
Cleanses me from the past
So when I make it out,

I'll absorb the life
She gives.
I'll start anew, and
Thank her every chance
I get.

Race
I catch opportunity as it
Whisks through the wind
I stand with my back
To the past.

I race the sun's light
To get as far
As I can
Each morning.
I cannot wait for those years
to catch up to me.
I must match the pace
Of the future.

Stamped
Hail storms
Pound the Earth.
They stamp the
Grasses into the
Dirt.
They despise to
See a standing
Structure;
So now we
Build again.

Arch
Reaching for the skies, she
Arches beyond our grasp,
Itching to see a
Newly cleansed world
Beneath the light
Of the star
We craved to be free once more.

duality

Fox
I struggle to laugh
Along with the fox,
When he snickers
So suddenly.
I never understand
His motivation.

What if I am the object
Of his amusement?

I chuckled anyway.

Horizon Lines
I keep running
Toward the line
Of the horizon
Over the mountains,
I can't help
But disregard the many
Horizon lines
Others have seen
Me hurdle.

New Moon
But, why does she hide
At the mere mention of her
Now becoming new?

Full Moon
My guide through the dark,
Who reminds me I am not
Alone in the night.

Sea Foam
When the tide comes in and she licks my toes
With her salty tongue, running sandy
Fingers through the
Creases between each digit, I must
Enjoy the sweet sensations
Before she ebbs away

Again.

New
If new were always preferred,
Would I still feel the tension
Of a knot beneath my ribs,
Pulling constantly until
I've doubled over,
Giving in?

Would my anxiety morph
Into excitement?

Would I be able to
Remind myself
I'm stronger than
The change?

Or would I always
Suffer knowing
It could always be
better?

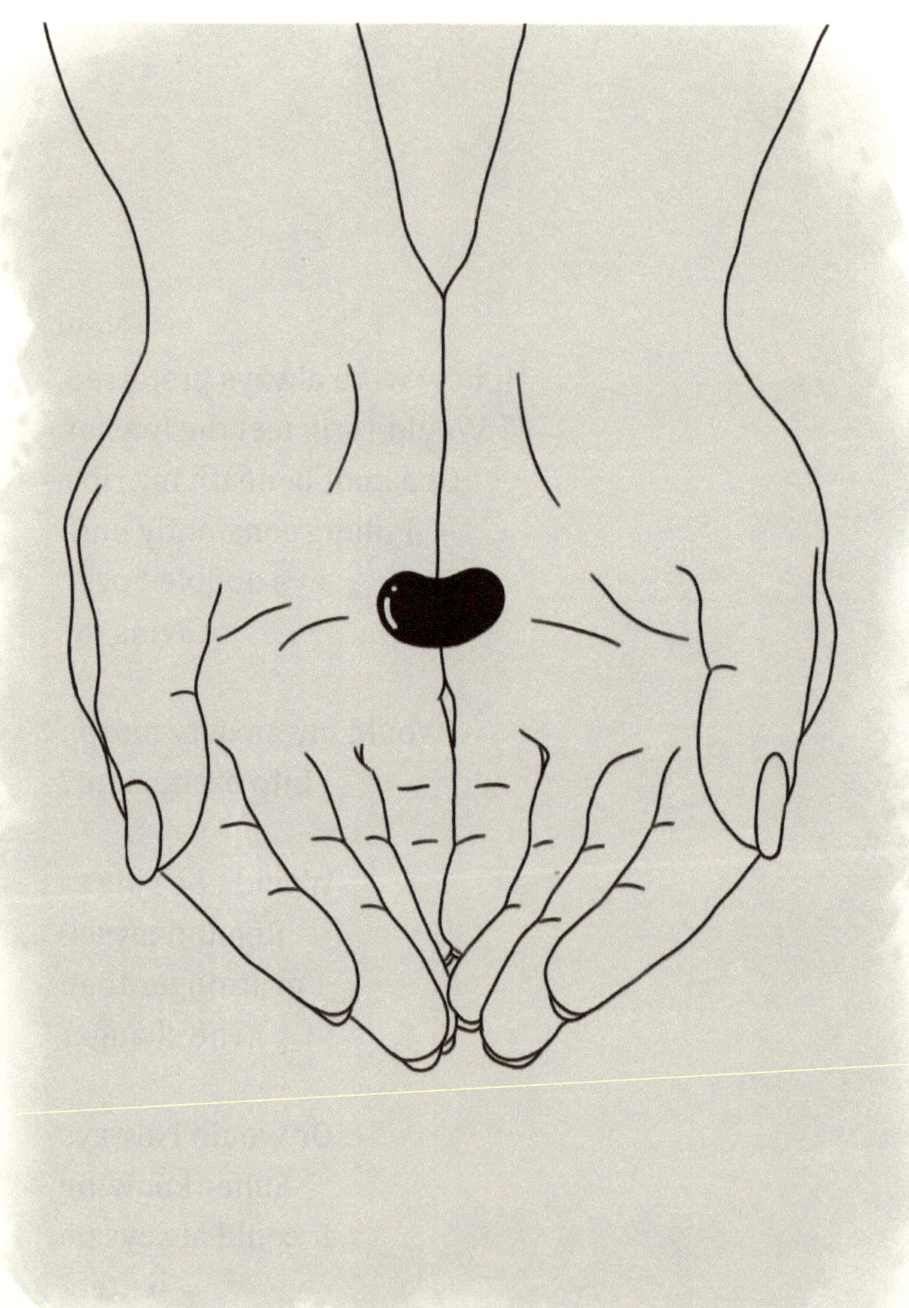

Time

February

Love

Glitter
For years after
The fact,
I'd still find tiny
Pieces of glitter
Hiding between the
Fibers of my carpet --
On my skin at the
Roots of my hair.
How many other tiny pieces
Of dust and plastic have been
Stashed in these small spaces,
Seemingly transcending time?

But I only ever see the glitter.

Tumbling Rocks
The rocks that tumble down
The mountainside
Beat the ridges into
Submission, smoothing out
Her texture after years
Of abuse.

Her defenses may rebuild
With time--

Or a well-swung hammer.

Sundial
Without a clock,
The sun will still report the time.
Shadows move in circles
Before they spread, and
Darkness reminds
The mortals on Earth
The axis stays
Spinning.

Daylight & Darkness
Her duties start before
The light breaks through the window panes.
Ambition's only timers are the streaks of
Sunlight over the walls.
But when she's done,
The patterns transform; speckled
In stardust
Over the clocks
Turned face down.

She wakes in the dark
She sleeps in the dark.
But the daylight misses her face.
Seems both are hot commodities.

Mid-Year Resolutions

We wake up, the first of the year
With renewed energy.
We intend to change;
We resolve
To be better than we once were
To achieve the dreams we left
Abandoned;

Buried deep in icy snow banks of years past
That melted with the warmth of spring
And dripped into the sewer grates,
Sinking further away, swept out of our lives.
Hidden in the septic tanks,
Flowing through pipes.

Still, water has memories.
It works in cycles, and always finds its way
Back to me.
A hot shower strikes with inspiration.
A glass from the tap before bed keeps me up at
night
For hours.

By then it's mid-February.
I've already failed my
New Year's Resolution.
Time and time again.
I can try
When the year is new again--
Once the universe is on my side.

Or I can try tomorrow
When the day is new again--
Because the universe
Brought these dreams back to me now

And she doesn't like to be kept waiting.

My Cup of Tea

It's a ceramic vessel
Filled with sad,
Dried, dull leaves.
Embraced in boiling liquids,
Those leaves unfurl;
They release their color;
They expand;
They perfume
The room.

It's a rusted kettle
Filled with boring,
Uninteresting, simple water.
Kissing the leaves,
That water absorbs;
It develops the color;
It accepts the flavor;
It becomes a thing
Of comfort.

When they mingle,
They make each other
Better.
More open.
More accepting.
They are more than
The sum of their parts.

You're the water.
I'm the leaves,
And together we're
My cup of tea.

A Choice
I thought it was a feeling.
Growing deep inside your gut

Trickling up into your heart
Trapping your brain until it slips

Soundlessly in every crack,
Keeping you up at night, stealing dreams,

Superseding every other care.
Effervescent, blithe, untroubled.

Damn if I wasn't fooled by the warmth,
Heating you now from within.

New love makes it easy to succumb,
But one day you'll hit a bump or two.

Over tears, you'll have to produce that love
Every day. Doubtlessly, and continuously.

You'll have to choose if this is worth the fight
Through uncertainty and darkness;

Savor a taste of that first moment, suck it up,
Push through, and decide to love again.

In the Stars
I will never say I'm over the moon,
I want to be out in the stars.

But still attracted to
Your gravity.

A Night In
Let's stay in, and be
Unapologetically
Ourselves together.

Aphrodite
Above the mountain
Peaks of Olympus,
Her beauty shines like
Rays of light
Onto the people far below.
Doubtless, she understands
Intuitively that she is lusted after-- valued
To society-- And yet she stays in with
Eros. Storge: True, familial love.

It Exists
If our love
Exists
In the minutes
Between phone calls
In the distance
Between our bodies
In the nights
Between waking moments
So, too, it can
Exist
In the anger
We feel
Together;
Within the space
We give
Each other;
In the heater
While we
Cool down.

To Make an End

War

March

Healing

The Role Model
I'm at war
with who I was,
who I am,
and who I'll be.

I want to be better.
I want to grow.
I want to
Love myself,

But

No one hates me
As much as I do

For everything
I have done
to another,

Which makes them
despise my
very existence,

I know
I've done worse;

I know
how bad I can get.

I forgive others
because it's so
much harder
to forgive
myself.

I'll love myself
so you can see.
I'll push myself
so I'll succeed.

I'm exactly the
role model
you'd hate
to be.

Glory
You're fighting the wrong fight.

You're dreaming of being lifted
Upon the strong shoulders of
The powerful,
For even just a minute,
And breathing the
Sweet nectars and
Splendors of success
Before they let you down

But what of the downtrodden?
They may be weak
But they are many.
And even when a few
Let you down,
There are hundreds
Behind them
To lift you
Up again.

Octopus
One arm holding the door,
One arm hiding his face,
One arm sweeping under the rug,
One arm directing me,
One arm deflecting blame,
One arm holding ground,
One arm keeping me down,
One arm
At my neck.

Control
A thick paddle brush
Through dampened hair
Pulls out wads--
Unkempt balls
Of strands
That matted--
Stretching out of their place
On my head.

--I'll suffer through pain if it means
Setting things right
Again.

It's nice to have
Control
At least once each day.

Insomnia
Is it possible
The world seems clearer
At night?
With your head on your
Pillow
With the
Quiet
All around you?
With the
Peace of blackness
Masking distractions?
Or perhaps
it's driven us
Mad;
Hiding truths
In shadowed corners
Where our
Private demons
Materialize.

Delusion and
Self doubt
Always shrivel
In the daytime--
So I'll keep
A small lamp
On.

Warm Again
I noticed
Loose threads and frayed edges
framing a little spot of skin underneath
Fleece-lined, black socks.

I grabbed a permanent marker
And colored over my skin
To fill in the hole.

It blended right in.

I've gotten so good at
Temporary fixes
And "Good Enoughs",

But it sure would be nice
To feel warm again.

Cycles
He washed my feet
So I could wash
Yet another.

Reciprocal
He loved me back
To feeling like myself.

I just want
To do the same.

Bleached
There are these yellow marks
On a well-loved, white blouse
In the back of my closet.

I sprayed it in chemicals, and
Let it sit for a few days.
Choking on fumes while it
Removed the stains.

I noticed the yellowing
Had greatly faded,
But the bleach
Had made a spot
On some new, black slacks.

*Repairs can be
So messy.*

Paper Dolls
I'm playing with
Paper dolls
So regularly that the
Edges have bowed
And the
Shapes have crumpled,

But if I
Play pretend
Enough
I might be able
To understand the
why.

It's time
I found some tape
To mend their rips.

Winding
She stopped at the divide,
another fork in the road,
spiraling deeper into a
lonely wood.
She huffed and pivoted
back around.

She must have followed
the wrong track.

But in an attempt
to redirect her journey,
she found that path
had circled back
to the divide which
drowned in black.

She needed to travel through
the intense darkness

to reach the light.

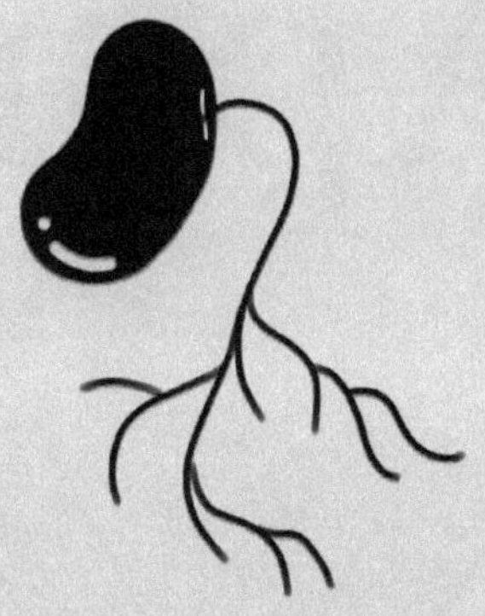

Rebellion

April

Betrayal

Productive

My brain is flooding with
Self-imposed responsibilities
And unrelenting guilt
For favoring rest
When it's needed.

How easy would it be
To start a
Mutiny in my mind?

To circumvent
These feelings of
Failure
When I grow
Feverish or fatigued?

I'm exhausted
And overwhelmed.
Am I worthless
For not expending
Every ounce of energy on
Productivity?

Escape
In a tiny
One by one cell,
I thought to conserve
My space.

I made myself small,
So my room
Might feel big.

But if I stand
And if I expand

I could be big enough to break
These walls
And escape.

Tumbleweed
I have been starved of water
So long, I'm dehydrated-
Drying-- dying.

I've been cut off
Like a tumbleweed,
Separated from its roots

Caught in the wind
Twisting and spinning
Out of control.

So I leave my seeds
As I go, and find
New places to grow.

Breathing
When I feel silenced,
I take long, deep breaths
With my mouth wide open
As if in a yawn

And I dare you to
Condemn me for breathing.

Even in silence,
You will know I'm there.

The Smart One

When I was young
I was told,
"You're the smart one,
Your sister is the pretty one."

"Right," I said.
Of course that's true.
Everyone has a gift,
I couldn't be greedy and have two.

I didn't think it was possible
For body image issues
To stem from intelligence
I thought I must commit to.

I always thought I had to choose.
So I'd look myself in the mirror everyday
And remind myself I'm ugly
So I could make my brilliance stay

And when I got my first C, I cried.
Suddenly I wasn't anything. It implied
I wasn't exceptional.
And being average wasn't acceptable.

I lost my gift, so
I let myself feel beautiful
For the first time
In years.

And in spite of my C,
I got my degrees.
And I start my mornings
By dressing in pink.

Because no matter
What people think
Or what they see
When they look at me

I know I'm more than vanity
I'll challenge their beliefs.

Intellect and beauty
Are not exclusive mutually.

betrayal

Clasped
When we held hands,
All I ever felt were the places
Where our knuckles brushed
And how the ridges of our fingerprints
Ran over ripples of smooth skin.
It was warm, and simple.

I didn't notice the gap
Between our palms
Where you intentionally separated from me
Until we started pulling apart.

Amputation
It was bad enough to know
I was losing a leg.

But did you have to
Saw it off
With a dull
Plastic knife?

The Back
You stabbed me
In the back
So you wouldn't have
To look me
In the eye.

Rose-Colored Glasses
My rose-colored glasses
are old.
They've grown dustier
as they've aged.

I keep
rubbing them clean,
But it seems
They're growing stained,

And everything
They once shown
So brightly around

Has darkened and
Deepened to an ugly
Shit brown.

Train
It's like being hit by a train.
You never see it coming.
There's no reaction time
There's no time to process.

One minute you're crossing
The railroad tracks

Then you're blinded by pain.
In every inch of your body
Vibrating. Pulsating.

And the train
Keeps going.

Canary Yellow
A bright little bird,
Singing songs of
Positivity, Joy, and Loyalty.

A sweet little friend
who brings you great
Honor, Creativity, and Intellect.

A lonely, jealous creature,
To remind you of
Cowardice, Betrayal, and Lies

Redemption
May
Hope

redemption

Windswept
The Wind can be unforgiving,
She can devastate the world
She leaves behind Her
In dust and
In rubble.

But then She ripples
Through your hair
And whips the
Strands into position
Perfectly, effortlessly.

And then She fills
You with air and
Pushes you forward
When you're feeling
Stuck in place.

It's almost like
The rest
Never happened.

Redeeming Qualities
It may not be perfect,
But at least
It's something.

Grace
I've been writing for
The Devil's Advocate
But
Not every villain
Deserves a redemption arc.

Under the Arch

A rainbow
Sprouted from
The patch of grass
Outside my window.

I could climb it
To reach the end
And revel in the
view above,

Or I can go
Under the arch.

I don't need
To be on top
To make it to
The destination.

Consistent
"What can I do?"
Is a tough question.

There is no one thing
You can do.

My trust
Cannot be bribed.
My trust
Cannot be bought.

Trust needs
Consistency.

Then we can rebuild.

Rock Bottom
Thud. She fell
To the Bottom
Of the Cavern.
On the rocks and
In the dark.

One misstep is
All it took
To find herself
Trapped
In the walls
With jagged edges
Threatening her
With shards
Of slate and
Stacked stones.

But it's exactly
That rough,
Unpolished surface
That allowed her
To climb her way
Out.

Waving

When I walk around the block and back,
I always pass the local retirement home
And wave to the old folks, who are strangers to
me
As I pass by. Across the street,

In full view from the balconies
Of this facility
Is a wholly unspecial playground
With a few swings

And jungle gyms
Where kids climb and spin.
I always pass them
And the kids wave to me

A stranger.

One time I walked right by,
It simply slipped my mind

I could hear a grumpy voice
Huff and say,
"People are so rude nowadays.
I remember when everyone waved."

I never forgot to wave
At the elderly strangers again
And I always wave back to the children
As they jump and flail in my direction.

And as I pass,
They wave behind me.
It's sweet to see
How much they believe

Everyone deserves acknowledging.

Hope
Help me stay more
Optimistic.
Please don't let me give up
Easily.

Dreams
I'll sleep on my back
So I can dream
Facing the sky

Anyway
Shooting stars
Don't stop
Racing
Across the
Sky.

You may
Not see them
On cloudy
Nights,
But they're
Always
There,
Skating behind
The fog,
Never being
Wished upon
So

Wish anyway.

Butterflies

These stomach bugs keep getting worse,
Laying eggs in the walls of my gut
Crawling around as caterpillars
Eating remnants of my breakfast and lunch,
Having me eye my supper anxiously.

And eventually, they'll wrap themselves in cocoons
And rest a day or two,
But when they break those outer shells,
Their wings will flap so hard
They beat me 'till I'm bruised.

All I can feel are these
Butterflies in my stomach,
And I hope they never leave.

Over the Bridge

It's a long walk
With rivers and creaks
Flowing with uncertainty
And fear below.

It's rickety, and broken,
With slats made of rotting
Wood and ropes covered
In mold.

Years of dust and grime,
Cracks and splits
Shaking back and forth
Until you're plagued
With vertigo.

But I built this bridge,
So I could get over it.

I know I'll feel at peace
Once I reach
The other side.

Unity
June
Joy

unity

The Birds
We may be smaller
But if we work together
We can swarm the crane

The Crane
What have I ever
Done but be different than
Others and exist?

Blue Jeans

He heard her heels click
Down the hall,
He followed close
Behind in the silent
Tap of tennis shoes
Against linoleum floors.

Her silky blouse billowed
In the breeze,
Whisking the smell of
Vanilla sugar through
The air around him.

His chiseled jaw
Cut through the air
Like knives as
He marched
Against the winds.

Her smile: bright
And white.
His hands: dark
And calloused.
And yet they both
Wore blue jeans.

Solidarity
It's hard to watch
A friend go dredging
Through the marsh.
When the wet stains
Could be from murky water
Or from a foul sweat.

So I'll follow,
And wet my socks
In solidarity.

No one should walk
Through water
Alone.

Compromise
I've been stubborn.
I've asked everyone to walk a mile
To come to me
Through the mountains,
Across the seas.

It takes practice.
That first step
Feels so far,
But I notice
It's made us closer.
The lines of your face
Have become clearer, and
I'm starting to see you
As you are.
'

If I take one step,
What's one more?
Then two.
Then three.
Then five.

Until we finally meet
In the middle.

The Sky
As a child, I'd often
Look to the sky.
Cloud gazing and
Stargazing.

I never really knew why
It was so appealing.
Then I realized.
The sky is
Vast, dabbled in
Unending patterns
Miles above my head
Littered with irregularities,
Yet still forming
One great,
Unified
Piece of art.

Even if I stand out,
I can still fit in
And be a part of something
Wonderful.

joy

Happy Place
Involuntary movements
Come from music
Thoughtless motions
When I feel broken
Keeps me dancing
Without planning

Just enough to keep expanding

Beats that make me
Bob my head keep
Bouncing while I lay in bed
When melodies
Flood memories
And harmonies,
Extremities

Endorphins start to rally
Before songs reach finales

Koi
They pass by each other
In weightless pools
Full of clear, fresh water
To cool their fins.

They ripple through
The water and
Soak up the colors
Of the sun
And moon
And clouds.

A perfect reflection
Of the world outside
Even in their ponds.

Dragonfly
Dipping and darting, he
Races the world
Around him.
Gazing past his crystalline,
Opalescent wings, he
Never falters or
Fails to display
Liveliness in every
Yard

Keeping Busy

Buzz.

A little honey bee
Keeping busy
He won't rest

Buzz.

He keeps on flying forward
Finding nectar
Spreading pollen

Buzz.

The worker bee loves his job;
He's quite pleased not to think.

Buzz.
He has no time to worry
When there's so much more to do.

Kaleidoscope
The scene through
A kaleidoscope
Seems so overwhelming
With infinite colors and shapes
Twisting in different directions
Yet I keep my eye glued to the lens.
I've been desperate for
A little more color.

Freedom
July
Growth

freedom

Hair
Sifting my fingers through your hair
And watching them slip between strands
Diving into the dense ocean of
Smooth, sandy-brown segments,
Breaking through the waves, marveling at
Fragments flaunting a brassy shine;
It reminds me so much of setting off down a hill
And running wildly through the field below--
Uninhibited, unrestricted.

I revel in knowing that
I'm the only one allowed
To let you come undone.

Cloudless & Shamrocks
After the rain, in the sky
A bright rainbow rises
Unhidden by the fogs
Of fuzzy cumulus clouds.

Attracted by the light show,
Hordes of hapless souls
Crowd around the grasses
Where the prism sprouts

From the ground
Like a sapling, like a tree.
To comb through
Fields of green

Seeking the single four-leaf clover.
Blessed by luck,
They might finally
Escape a cycle of
Misfortune.

What a shame
There can only be one.

Training Wheels

Training wheels are never quite as steady
As two arms.
Arms can bend and angle just so
To hold me upright on this bicycle.

Training wheels can't push me along
Like you have.
Guarding me at my
Front and back.

Training wheels can't push me faster
You've sent me, full speed along my path
So I can get where I'm going
In record time.

Training wheels can't push me farther,
And by the time you've released me,
I'm flying, finally, to travel the road
That I can only travel alone.

Training wheels offer balance,
Support, and maybe a little comfort,
But you've given me the strength to ride alone
And because of you, I know I'll be alright.

Fire
I play with fire
Constantly, if I don't I
Fear I'll freeze in place.

Tick, Tock
I'm a slave to sleep

I want to writhe through
The untouched, moonlit hours
And experience freedom

From lost time.

Phoenix
I'm following the heat,
Like a sunflower's face,
Chasing the sun.

The phoenix can be reborn
By passing through flames.
Surely, so can I.

If the flames are bluer, whiter,
Taller or wider,
Will I come out stronger?

Or does it matter?

For I know I'll be free
On the other side.

growth

Criticism
I don't know if I take Criticism well.
She comes spitting at you like
Knives; cutting through
Tension in the air,
Waiting in anticipation
For a slice.

A cut in the ear that burns for days,
Repeating whispers of words She said.
A slash through the mind that made
Pointed choices.
A mark in the hands
That created.
Little scars
And reminders
That ache when I
Go back to create.

But I've learned from Her.
I can take Criticism,
And I can apply Her.
But damn, she sure
Does hurt.

Perennials
I don't expire in
My off-season. Just a rest,
And I'll grow fuller.

Grow
Go on and
Reap the benefits
Of all the
World around you

The Roots of the Past
My can keeps running out of water.
So much is needed to reach the deepest roots
Of my oldest plants.
They've grown so big, and overwhelming,
Thick, and thorny
Selfishly drinking in all the sunlight
This garden receives.

I'm starting to wonder
If I'll ever see the new seeds sprout.
If all my resources are spent
On what my garden once was,
I'll never know what she will be.

Peaks and Valleys

She sees the path to the top of the cliffs,
But never the destination.
Her eyes stay steady and forward.
She climbs constantly, endlessly
But succumbs to curves, bends,
And valleys in her way.

It stoops so low, and the top seems
Just as far from her as ever.
Yet when she finally looks behind her,
Considering heading back,
She sees how far she's come,
And slides right down into that canyon
So she can push on.

The trail is never a straight shot,
But it always looks up eventually.

Treehouse
My branches are winding
Around and around
Forming natural barriers
Against the elements.
I've grown so much;
My skin's so thick,
Tough, and ragged
The way bark should be.
Easy to climb, difficult to tear down--

I want you to
Build your treehouse here.

I can protect you now.

Conflict
August
Power

conflict

The Main Character

I wonder how many tales
Or stories by friends of friends
Have started with "This woman I know..."
And that woman has been me.

How many times have I been the protagonist?
And does that number outweigh the
Number of times I've been
The villain?

To someone, I'm the hero
Who defended the meek
Who extended a lifeline
In a time of need.

To another, I'm an abuser
Who beat down the strong
Who held ambitions back
And felt no remorse.

The only thing I know is true is
Even the truth is subjective.

Imposter Syndrome
I think I am an imposter.

I have closets lined with hats and masks
And facts that allow me to act
like I'm someone new.

Someone successful.
Someone I am not.

I could be an imposter.

I have twelve-page resumes
To prove I am who I say--
With lines that embellish the truth.

Someone of value.
Someone I am not.

I might be an imposter.

I have walls of trophies and plaques
Glittering and attracting attention to
my achievements.

Someone talented.
Someone I am not.

I am an imposter.

I have a performance I put
on every day; I've become such
a good actor.

Someone notable,
Although I am not.

Man vs Nature
In times of drought,
She'll pray for rain;
So much, it'll flood
Up to her knees.
So hard, it'll leave welts
Over her arms.

Of course
It'll hurt,
But that would be
Better
Than this

Different
What no one mentions to you
About being different
Is that while you
Revel in finally
Becoming yourself
You always have to
Keeping looking
Over your shoulder.

The miserable are never content
Being miserable on their own.
They'll drag you through
The pits of hell
To sit
Alongside them.

The Dark Side
It was nearing the close. I could tell.
I knew we would end before we began,
But I was overdue
For a mistake.

He asked me if I'd like to go for
A walk in the woods.
I said yes.
I had space for one more good memory.

So we hopped over day-old puddles,
And stepped on leaves
Which disappointed me
With minimal crunch.

"Look up," he said, directing my attention
To a wide, silver moon,
peeking out behind the mangled branches
of a dozen trees overhead.

"Do you know what shape it is?" He asked.
Inquisitive.
"A sphere," I answered.
Matter-of-fact.

He chuckled for a brief moment;
It was a brief moment too long.
"Wrong," he replied.
I hate that word.

"That's a waning gibbus," he said in a certain
tone.
It could have been playful,
But it felt condescending.
A father talking down to his child.

"The moon is a sphere," I dug my heels
Into the mud.
I could feel it creeping up to my ankles,
Wet and dirty,
I held my ground
Defiantly.

He stopped with me,
And took a step back to
Look me in the eye.
"You knew what I meant."

Evidently, I'm too stupid to know
A waning gibbus,
But I am smart enough
To read his mind.

In spite of all his charm,
I could see in this moment
Exactly why we were never meant to be.
He lived in the moments with me
He saw the moon as it was.

But I could see the bigger picture,
I saw the truth hidden in the shadows.

I knew we would end before we began;
I've always been able to see
The dark side of the moon.

power

Listening
It was not enough to simply
Be seen.
I wanted to be
Audible.
It took too long to learn--
I'd rather have ten
Friends who
Listen
Over a million
Followers who merely
Hear.

Mountaintop
It looks so final, and absolute.
The peak of the mountain.
Pointed, harsh, and jagged.
But the ground up there is just flat
As the plains below,
Though it doesn't stretch as wide.
It feels so very similar, only
It's much lonelier there
At the top.

Marie
They called me Marie--
Marie Antoinette.

When they said
They had no bread.
I offered to share
My cake.

But it seems they misread
So they cut off my head.
I've paid for their
Mistake.

Warriors

When I think of great leaders,
I've never pictured figureheads
Perched atop a golden throne
Drenched in waves
Of sparkling jewels
Like starlight
Kissing their fingers
Under each flicker of light.

I imagine warriors, with dirty hands,
And worn shoes that tells tales
Of long, arduous journeys.
Scars that trim their faces
Like the ripped edges
Of lace.

Those who shine in the day
And in the night.

Crowns that show through
Their eyes
And not balancing atop
Their heads--
Ready to topple at
A moment's notice.

Royalty which does not
Beseech the poor to bow before them,
But keeps them at their ears
And truly hears.

Lords and Ladies that
Stand beside their people.
And are empowered by
Their strength.

Electricity
Electrify me.
Wake me up.
Start the lightning running
Through my veins.
Sizzling my blood with
Trails of power and
Productivity.
Plug me in to a
Power bank of
Motivation.

Watch me
Light up the room

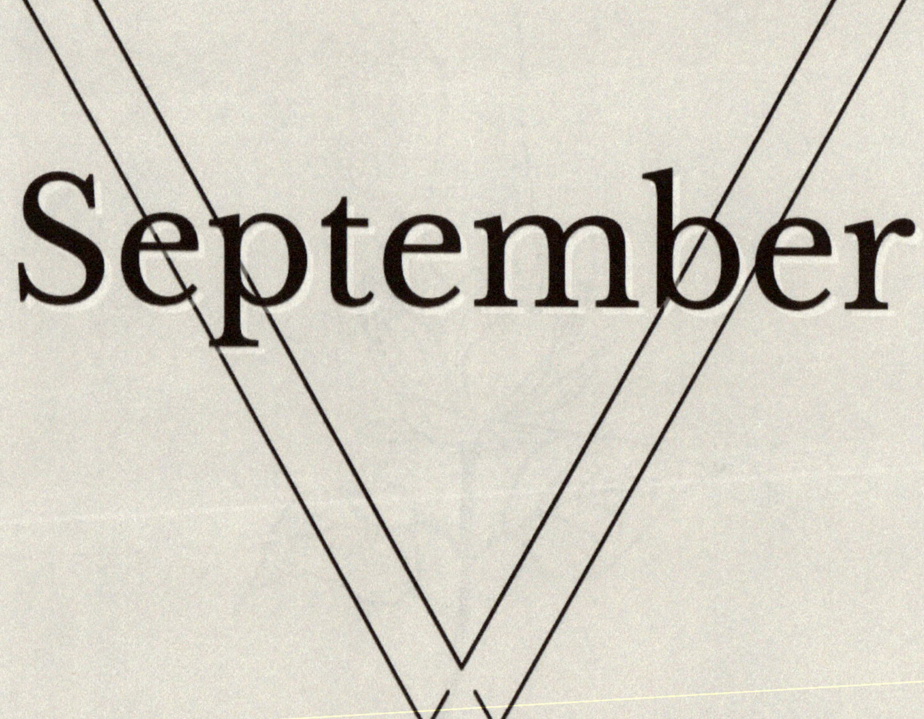

Wisdom
September
Judgment

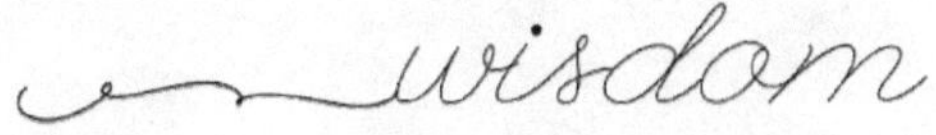

Wild

The wild horses
Trot along the coast
While sweet sea breezes
Comb their manes.

They know the value
Of trotting along,
But they're never afraid
To stop and rest.

They let the sounds
Of crashing waves
Wash over them,
And get up again

When the time is right.
The path will be ahead
Waiting for them.

They never go back
Over their hoofprints.

The High Road
The sunlight reflects
Against the high roads.
Causing blind forgiveness,
There are no boundaries
At the edges of the cliffs,
And a risk of falling off
Again.

But the low roads sink
Into the cliffside
And fester in darkness
Of petty grudges
And hate.

I think I'll stay the course between,
Where the sun's warmth is absorbed
So I can feel a little love
For myself for once.

Blades
He sat in a field,
Surrounded by green.
Whether an act of hate
Or jealousy,
He couldn't resist--
He clenched in his fist
A clump of fluffy blades,
and when he looked back
To see the damage he'd done
He couldn't quiet tell
From where he pulled.

What a waste
Of energy.

Wrong
They said,
"You're wrong."
I said,
"Okay, and?"
"And you should be ashamed."

"So, what do I do?"
"Be better."
"But how?"
"Well, you should know by now."

It seems so insane
How I get all the blame
From teachers who won't teach
And leaders who won't lead-
They play games of projection
Rather than self-reflection.

At least I've taught myself
What not to do.
So I can say I learned
Something.

Natural
I'm pleased to say
I have no natural talent.
I've learned every
Skill I have.

I was never good
The first time around,
So I learned to fix
My mistakes.

I've found value in practicing
The wrong way to do things

So I know what it looks
And feels like.

So I will know
When I've failed.

The naturals
Never can tell.

judgement

Hardbound
She is a
A novel.
Deep.
Complex.
She will not bend
Until you get inside.
She could be flexible.
She'll move.
She'll flip.
But you'll
Have to break into
That harsh exterior.
You'll have to look past
The hard cover
And read
Between the lines.

Weather
Each morning
I check outside
The window.
I want to know
What the weather is like.

As if the sun and clouds
Will be an indicator
For my mood,
And foretell
Significant events.

As if the fog
Will give me the power
To decide what lies ahead
Today.

The sun does not control
The Earth,
And the rain does not
Control me.

I don't need
The weather's
Validation.

Proverbs
He doesn't want to know.
He doesn't care to know.
His questions aren't a means
To understanding.
His questions aren't a quest
For knowledge.
He only wants
To make you look
As stupid
As he feels.

Law
I'll continue to argue, even when
You've already decided
I'm the criminal.

Judge
Justification of
Ugliness
Described as
Goodness and
Earnestness

So Far
Stop saying
That was
The best day
Of your life.

It was
The best day
Of your life
So far.

There must be something
Better ahead.
Otherwise,
What's the point?

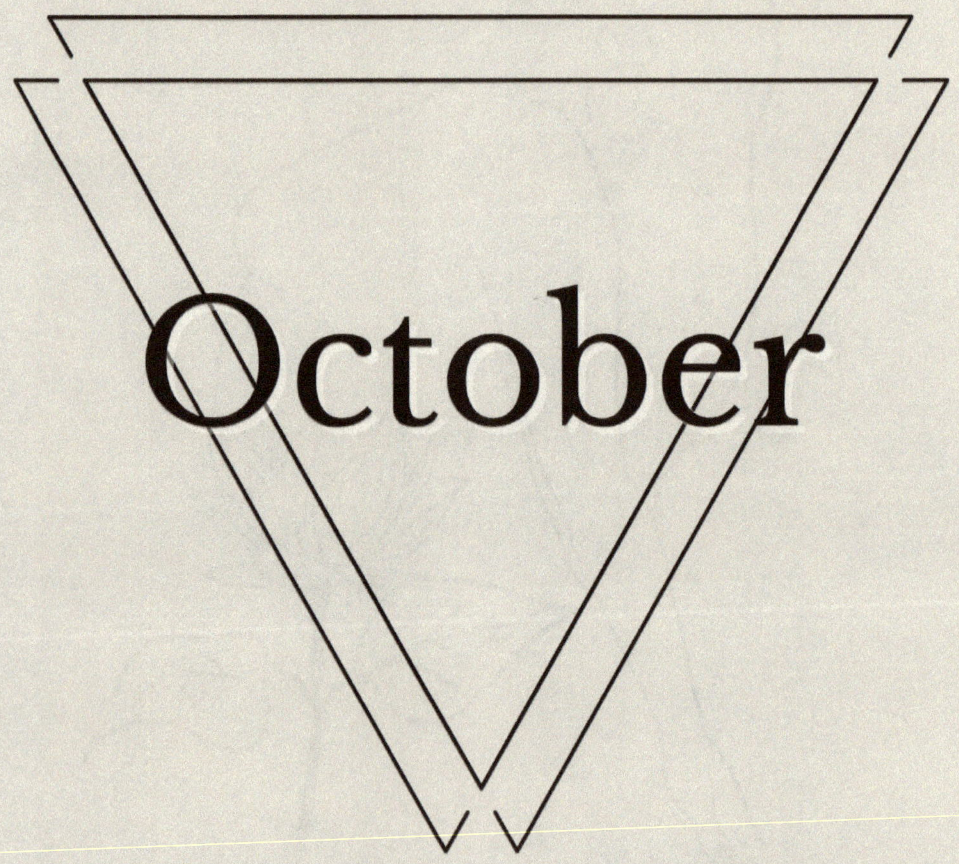
Passion
October
Manifestation

passion

Word Carver
Writing
Is much like
Sculpting.

Both are messy,
ugly, and uninviting
In the process.

The first draft is stone
Or the clay, largely unshaped,
Amorphous and rough.

It isn't until the editing,
When you add in the details
And remove the extraneous that

The vision
Reveals itself
From within.

Cravings
I craved the beautiful
Visions in my head,
But with the colors blending--
The lines curling--
The shapes blurring--

They felt so out of reach.

Highlights and shadows
Were all I knew for certain.
Lined up just so--
Appearing only
On the backed
Of my eyelids.

I wanted to see something
Beautiful
In a world that looked so
Ugly.

A craving on satisfied
By pencil and paper,
Paint and canvas,
Color and imagination.

A rumble from within--
I was hungry to create

Art.

A Letter
Do you remember
That day
We danced
In the rain?
I'm still pretending
It was yesterday.

Every now and then
Memories
Have me reliving
Fantasies.
But it never
Was your company
That stuck
With me;

It was always
About the dancing.

Volcanic Spirit
It doesn't need
To erupt
And shroud
The atmosphere
With ash,
Or burn so hot
It hurts.

It can be
A slow ooze
From within,
Leaving evidence of
Its existence
From a safe distance

To be marveled at
For years
To come.

Good
I've gotten
Good
At a lot,
But
I've never been
Great
At anything.

I can't commit
To just one talent,
And spend
Every waking moment
Becoming
Great
When there's so
Much more to do
And love.

So I guess
Good
Is
Good Enough.

manifestation

Echoes

Maybe you don't agree,
But it doesn't matter.
I'll keep screaming affirmations
Into caves and caverns
And listen to the echoes
Tell me
How incredible I am.

Falling
I've grown so tired
Of myself.
My green
In my leaves
Has faded.
Replaced
By oranges
And yellows.
I'm not
The best version
Of myself
Anymore.
So I will
Drop these leaves
One by one;
Leave the old
And dry behind.
And come back
Better again.

Come What May
She'd heard
The snowstorm
Was ahead.
She'd felt
The chill
From miles away.

She could not
Stop a blizzard.
Through brawn
Or bribes.

She had to sit
And wait.
For the snowfall
To arrive.

And as it rounded
Bends, trailing crystals
At its heels,
She sighed.
Knowing this was
Meant to be

She loosened up
Her shoulders
And chose to let it come.
She knew the snow
Would be lovely,
After everything went numb.

When she bowed her head to destiny,
She opened the gates to peace.

Deserved
Did I commit a mortal sin
In another life?
Did I offend Zeus
By falling in love
with the wrong man?
Could I have cut off a friend
Who aches deeply for revenge?
Or maybe I cut off
A spiteful woman in traffic?
Could I have been so selfish,
Stubborn,
And cruel
That karma has made a
Full rotation back to me?

Do I deserve
This?

Match
No one else
Will do it for you.
If you find
You've become
Stagnant
And you aren't
Moving forward,

Strike a match
And light the fire
Under your own ass.

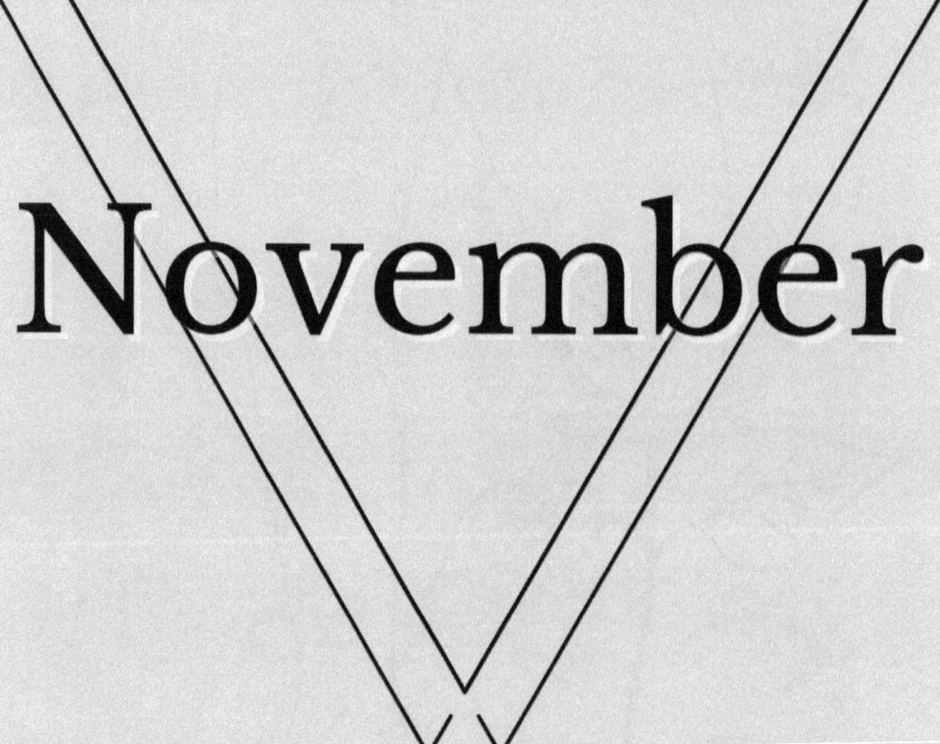

Honesty
November
Transition

Transparent
The window isn't transparent
If you keep the curtain drawn.

Promises
Honesty
Divided by
Consistency
Equals the
Reliability
Of your promises.

A Sense of Direction
I didn't know,
which road to take.
They both seemed
Perfectly fine
At a glance.
I made the
Right
Which turned out
To be
Wrong.
My sense of
Direction, perhaps
Isn't the best.
And while
They both seemed
Perfectly fine
At a glance,
I drove in circles
For hours.

Keeping my
Destination in mind
Didn't mean
I could avoid
The consequences.

Please Stand Up
I'll stand up
When you call
My name,
No matter the
Cause.
I own
Being myself--

Every
Faux
Pas

Humiliated
I've never felt more
Humiliated
Or heard more
Laughter
Than when I had been
Honest
With the world.

I've never found
Myself
That funny.

High Definition
The truth is
I haven't changed;

I've always been
Like this.

It just took
A few years

For the pixels
To fall into place.

I am the same,
Only now I'm in

High Definition.

transition

Clean Slate
I want a clean slate.

I want to suck up
All the dust and dirt
Around me and
Breathe pure air
A while.

It's strange
How once I've
Finally found my place
The dust begins
To settle again.

And the dirt
Will pile higher
And higher
In the same places
It used to.

Things only
Stay clean
With effort.

Clean slates
Get filthy quickly.

Pastels
Oil pastels
Leave textures behind
Like waxier,
Messier,
Crayons.
But
A little pressure
Smudging pigments
Helps
Fill in
The cracks.
Transforming
The draft
To the final
Work.

Honey
With lips
Slightly parted
She keeps
Drooling
Rivers
Of honey
And nectar,
Until her body
Is coated
In sweet
Sticky
Liquids,
As though
It will
Make the
Change
She wants
To see.

Honey isn't
Magic.

Some changes
Can't be
Seen.

If the Leaves Aren't Green
The storm had erupted in a matter of seconds.
I stood beneath tiny droplets, beating me down,
steadily pounding me into the ground,
surrounding me with falling oranges and browns.

I found shade under the leaves of a big, strong tree,
but as quickly as the water fell, so did his leaves.
I let him shield me until he was left bare.

So, too, I left.

I forced myself through pain, and again, attempted
finding salvation by
another.
She smelled like pine, fresh and clean. I reached to
hold her trunk, but
she was guarded, barbed.

Needles pressed into my skin.
I stood outside of her and stared into the sky, letting
beads of acid touch my lips.
I whispered, "Let it rain."

I took notice once more with the bare tree, weathering
the storm as I did.
I pushed myself through the winds that blew me back
and wrapped my arms
around him.

Archery
Arrows soar
Through the air
Sharp and smooth.

They cut between
Currents to reach
Their targets.

The pathway
To the mark is
Always a
Straight shot.

I wanted that,

But arrows
Don't adapt
To the moving world
Around them.

They're stuck
On their route
Until they reach
The target

Or until it gets stuck
In a tree.

Evolution and
Archery
Are simply not that
Easy.

Trust

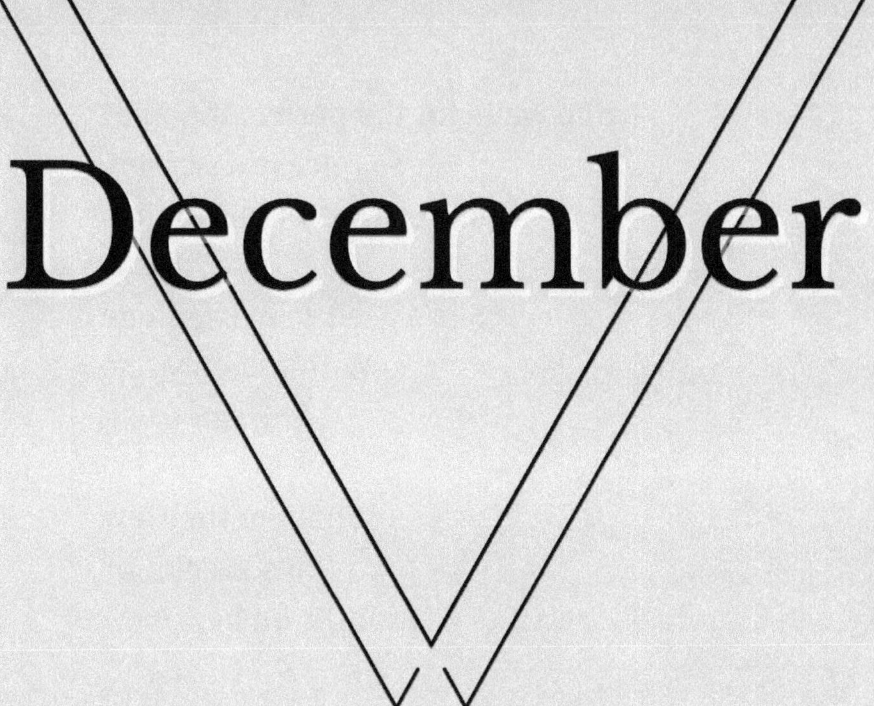
December

Completion

trust

Mountain Lion
She stalks through the
hills, through the valleys
And the trees.

She waits for the perfect moment
To release a scream,
But no paws come running.

She's used to being alone
With the only one
She can trust.

What another few
Days, weeks, or
Months on her own?

It's better to wait
For the right partner
Than to settle.

Trust
Toppled into
Ruin by the first sign of foulness
Uttered. Regardless of how
Sorry you might be, you've
Taken off your mask.

Embrace
I'll never mistake
The feeling of warmth off your
Skin for protection.

Trader
The trader walked
With his arms
Behind his back,

Collecting puddles
Of offerings
At his feet,

But never
Presenting anything
In return.

I want
To see
Your hands,
Trader.

What are
You hiding
From me?

Calloused fingers
Of a hard-working man,
Or the supple skin
Of a swindler?

Palms can be
So telling
If you know
How to read.

Magnets
Someone said to me recently,
They didn't understand why
My best friend is
My best friend.

She's so friendly,
intuitive, and
positive.

While

I'm so shrewd,
logical, and
cynical.

There are two
Fundamental reasons,
I think.
First, we both speak about others
In the same way.
Realistic, honest,
And respectful;
Even through
Our frustrations.

I have never once thought
She'd speak ill of me with
My back turned.

And then second,
We're both grossly
Ambitious and motivated.
We get so easily swept up
In our hopes and dreams,
We often forget to call
And check in.

Yet, every time I call,
She is happy to hear from me.
And I, her.

I keep her grounded,
She keeps me open-minded.
Like magnets,
Even when we separate,
We find ways back together.

Trampoline
Kiss my bruised knee
And help me to my feet.
Bounce me back to the top
Like a trampoline.

I know I will fall again.
And I know you will catch me.

Milkshake
I sucked on the
Straw for hours
Trying to indulge in
The last drop
But no matter how I
Sipped and slurped
It always dripped
Back out into
The base
Of the glass.

I suppose
I'll never be
Finished.

Rituals

I have two daily rituals bookending my time in bed.

In the morning, when I wake up, I hit the snooze button three times.

On weekdays, I make my coffee.

On weekends, I make my tea.

I shuffle and pull a card from a tarot deck to orient myself for the day.

Today, my card represented community and taking care of one another.

I checked my horoscope too, it said to keep pushing forward.

I need a little direction to keep me motivated throughout the days.

But the evenings are a little different.
In the evening, I massage creams into my face
as some semblance of self-care.
I reflect on all I accomplished, and affirm
myself in the mirror.
I subtract three snoozes from the time I need
to be awake and set my alarm.
Finally, I put in my headphones, and I cover my
eyes in a mask,
If I don't, my brain will keep me up all night
telling me how much more I could have done.
And after an hour or two of drowning out my
insecurities, I eventually fall asleep.

Then I'll wake up to hit my snooze button
three times.

Chains
She kept
Linking chains
In succession,

In a strand
So long
It wrapped
Twice around
The Earth.

She could go around again,
Or
Just connect the ends.

Stumbled
Not every remarkable moment
In life
Is bookended by
Remarkable journeys.

Sometimes
You just happen
Upon yourself.

I Did It
Here come the snowflakes
Stopping the rivers and
Freezing the lakes.

Whoever said it's
Impossible to
Walk on water?

I did it once
And I'll do it again.

Acknowledgements

This is now officially book number three for me. I created my first collection of poetry, *Where Flowers Bloom*, two years ago, followed shortly by my debut novel, *Fake it Till You Make It*, last year. This project was wildly different from my first collection though, because I already had years and years of poetry I had written to fill the pages, and such a clear-cut vision of what I wanted that collection to be and represent.

For my novel, I was so passionate about the story I was telling, and it was so deeply connected to myself and my own journey that the words came fairly easily. However, there is something so uniquely difficult about writing a collection of completely new poetry, making this, undoubtedly, the most difficult project I've completed to date. There was no initial concept, just a handful of inspiration and a hodge-podge of pieces I'd developed late at night before falling asleep which I quickly published in my Notes app as I was working on Fake It.

The concept for the book took so long to nail down. I started and scrapped so many ideas and artworks that I genuinely began to wonder if I'd ever finish. As always, it was my incredible support system of friends, family, and fellow writers who pushed me through the rough patches.

To start, probably the highest degree of thanks goes to Kaleigh Ceci, who honestly helped bring the vision back. When indecision and a flood of ideas is starting to take over your world and overwhelm you, sometimes you just need a friend to tell you, "You should make the book cover yellow," to really help things fall into place. Finally, I could see the pieces coming together inside that yellow cover. The topics, the theme, the story. It all started to make sense again. Small acts of kindness really do pay off. That is, of course, not to play off the large act of kindness she'd done which was participating in my beta reading phase and providing super helpful and meaningful feedback.

Thanks in this area also goes to my husband, Nick, who has never once told me no when it came to reading something or giving an opinion on little things like whether or not I should paint the nails in the art pieces.

As always, I'd also like to thank my family who supports me almost blindly through anything I do. They may never read this sentence in their (signed) copies of my books, but they are absolutely appreciated for being a constant in my life.

Until the next one!